GREGORY ELMAN

# Mental Health Self-Management for the Ones You Love

This book was professionally typeset on Reedsy.
Find out more at reedsy.com

# Contents

# 1

# Disclaimer

The information provided in this book, "Mental Health Self-Management for the Ones You Love," is intended to offer general guidance and support for individuals and their loved ones seeking to better understand and manage mental health challenges. However, it is essential to recognize that this book does not substitute for professional mental health care, evaluation, or treatment.

This book provides general information about mental health and self-management strategies. It does not cover every aspect of mental health conditions, and the information provided does not encompass all available options for mental health self-management.

Information in this book concerns primarily the author's understanding of mental health only in the United States of America. The contents of this book cannot replace the therapeutic work you might get from individual and/or group sessions with a helping professional. This book is not dispensing medical advice. Not all of the strategies in this book will work for everyone.  There are numerous suggestions for self-help in this book, yet the author realizes that you have to find the interventions that work for you because you are unique. After all, we have our own needs and preferences, such as the foods and drinks we consume (not everyone loves mint chocolate chip ice cream and pumpkin spice beverages), pets (dogs, cats, reptiles, etc.), entertainment choices (movies, music, books, sports, etc.), and whether we prefer to vacation at the beach or in the mountains.

The content of this book is not a substitute for professional mental health advice, diagnosis, or treatment. It is imperative that you consult with a qualified mental health professional or medical practitioner for personalized assessment and intervention tailored to your specific needs or the needs of your loved ones.

The author advises the readers to seek medical advice prior to engaging in physical activities and breathing exercises suggested in this book. For those unable to perform certain tasks, the author has found no modification at this time.

The author urges you to seek help from a professional mental health provider to gain insights unique to your situation and to work on recovery. Every person's mental health journey is unique. The strategies and insights presented in this book may not be suitable or effective for everyone. Individual circumstances, conditions, and experiences differ, and what works for one person may not work for another.

*Crisis Information*

If you or someone you know is in immediate danger, experiencing severe distress, or having thoughts of self-harm or harm to others, please seek emergency assistance immediately. Call 911 or go to the nearest emergency room.

In the USA, a person can call 911 for when you or someone you care for is at risk, specifically when you or the other person intend harm on self or harm to others (suicide risk or homicide risk). Typically the 911 operator will dispatch emergency services to the person's location. It is also possible for a person to present voluntarily to a hospital emergency department for suicidal or homicidal risk. There are several other circumstances when you need to call 911, such as fires, serious accidents, serious medical problems, crimes in progress, drug or medication overdose, etc.

International Association for Suicide Prevention has a website that may help you find help outside of the United States. Their website is https://www.iasp.info/suicidalthoughts/

In the USA 988. The website is 988lifeline.org for the 988 suicide and crisis lifeline, which was established because easier to remember than the previous number 1-877-273-8255. Deaf and hard of hearing people can gain access over text message to 988 or use 988 Videophone, or if preferred dial 711 for the relay relay service to 988.

IPV Intimate Partner Violence- https://www.thehotline.org/ or 1-800-799-7233 (SAFE). TTY is 1-800-787-3224. Or text "START" to 88788.

Child abuse reporting in the USA: If you suspect that a child is being abused or neglected, or if you are a child who is being mistreated, call 800-422-4453 immediately.

https://childcare.gov/consumer-education/child-protective-services#:

~:text=If%20you%20suspect%20that%20a,800%2D422%2D4453%20immediately

Elder abuse reporting in the USA: Your state will have its own reporting system, however, there is a nationwide reporting system on the internet: https://www.napsa-now.org/

The author, publisher, and distributors of this book are not liable for any actions taken by individuals or their loved ones based on the information presented herein. The responsibility for seeking appropriate mental health care and making informed decisions about treatment rests solely with the reader.

By reading this book, you acknowledge that you have read and understood this disclaimer and agree to its terms.

Remember, seeking professional guidance is often the most effective way to address mental health concerns. This book is meant to complement, not replace, the assistance provided by qualified mental health professionals. Your well-being and the well-being of your loved ones are of utmost importance, and seeking professional help when needed is a sign of strength and self-care.

# 2

# Introduction

Hello, and welcome to mental health self-management for the ones you love. You find yourself now in a unique position: the role of caregiver, friend, or family member to someone we love who is battling mental illness. This role is one of profound significance, marked by empathy, compassion, and unwavering support. Yet, it can also be daunting, emotionally draining, and at times, utterly bewildering.

I am pleased and excited that you have chosen this book to assist you with supporting a person or people in your life that you care about very much. I offer kudos and praise for taking this step to support your person, persons, or yourself. Whether you are a parent, spouse, sibling, friend, or mentor, this book can be your starting point on the journey of supporting someone you hold dear through their mental health struggles.

You, also, are completely worthy of love and support. The reason you can use this book for yourself could be simple self-preservation, yet the hope is that you and your special person will both heal and thrive. Remember, when you are in the airplane listening to the safety instructions, the flight attendant says, "Be sure to secure your own mask before assisting others." Essentially, take care of yourself so that you will be able to take care of others. If you are sleep-deprived, ignoring your hygiene, eating only processed foods, and ignoring your own mental and physical health needs, then how are you going to be at your best to provide good support to someone else? Please keep yourself safe and healthy. From here on in the book, I will be addressing both the mental health self-management supporters and the supported loved ones seeking mental health self-management; you know who you are.

Here you are. You are a brave person to help another human being to face the challenges of a mental illness. If you bought this book for yourself, I take my hat off to you for your bravery to charge into the battle to improve your mental health.

Wishing you wellness!

# 3

# What do you mean, "self-management?"

"If you know the enemy and know yourself, you need not fear the result of a hundred battles. If you know yourself but not the enemy, for every victory gained you will also suffer a defeat. If you know neither the enemy nor yourself, you will succumb in every battle."
— Sun Tzu, The Art of War

One could say that good mental health means feeling emotionally and mentally well. It's when you can handle stress, have positive relationships, feel good about yourself, and cope with life's ups and downs in a healthy way. It's like having a sturdy and contented mind and the ability to function well in your life.

Mental health self-management refers to the ability to take charge of your own mental well-being, making conscious efforts to maintain and improve it. It involves adopting positive habits, seeking support when necessary, and learning to cope with life's challenges in a healthy manner, such as in your personal and social life, at work, and in your learning environment. This concept is comparable to taking responsibility for the health of your body by eating well and exercising. Just as you can influence your physical health, what you do and think can also have a significant impact on your mental health.

Why is Mental Health Self-Management Important?

Mental health self-management is a vital aspect of overall well-being. It involves taking responsibility for your mental health, adopting positive habits, and seeking support when needed. By practicing mental health self-management, you can learn to manage your emotional well-being, build your resilience, enhance your self-awareness, and let go of the stigma surrounding mental health issues. Remember that taking small steps each day to care for your mental health can lead to significant improvements in your overall quality of life. So, start today by prioritizing your self-care, managing your stress, and seeking social and professional support. Your mental health matters, and you have the power to learn to do mental health self-management.

Another way to see it is that mental health self-management is about learning to use your individual resources to get yourself through an unpleasant or uncomfortable feeling or emotional experience, until the time when you can see a qualified mental health professional. Routine appointments may take days or weeks before you have your first appointment. Here, we are talking about experiencing things that disrupt your life such as getting upset, angry, depressed, afraid, stuck, anxious, stressed, disorganized, impulsive, sleepless, etc. The source, or the trigger mechanism, can be either internal, such as a thought you had or an internal physical sensation in your body, such as a queasy feeling in your stomach. The source, which can sometimes be called "triggers," which set off unpleasant and uncomfortable feelings and emotions. A trigger could equally come from your environment, such as something you see, hear, touch, smell, taste, or the use of alcohol or drug use (by the way, drugs can be street drugs, misused over-the-counter medicine, misused or abused prescription medicine, or various plants or mushrooms).

This side note is a message of discouragement regarding self-medicating instead of seeking the help of a medical professional for treatment for psychological pain and/or physical pain. Self-medication is the misuse or abuse of any number of legal substances (such as alcohol, over-the-counter medications, prescription medications, or prescription cannabis in some locations) or illegal substances is what people call "self-medicating." Other examples of over-the-counter (sold without a prescription) products are cold or cough medications. Some pre-scription medications are opioids (examples are Oxycodone, Oxymor-phone, Morphine, Codeine, Fentanyl, Hydromorphone, Tapentadol, or Methadone). Some prescribed attention deficit medications are amphetamines (Adderall or Dexedrine) or Methylphenidate. Examples of some illegal street drugs are cocaine, crack, methamphetamines, heroin, fentanyl, etc. Self-medicating is NOT self-management. Self-medicating is usually a symptom of psychological pain (for example, depression, anxiety, Post-Traumatic Stress Disorder (PTSD), etc.) or sometimes an untreated physical pain (for example, headaches or injuries to the body). Self-medication may be diagnosable as a substance use disorder (SUD), which is a serious medical condition that can be treated with professional interventions at a hospital, clinic, or private medical provider. People may self-medicate instead of finding professional treatment because of stigma or other reasons. A key point here is that SUD is a medical condition, NOT a moral failing. If you find yourself in this situation, please seek medical attention at your earliest opportunity. Resources to start pointing you in the direction of recovery can be found in the Resources section at the end of the book.

About triggers…

Here are a few examples of external triggers:

Seeing: Someone scratched the paint of your brand-new car, so your anger is triggered. You see your cheating ex-partner in the grocery store, so you become embarrassed and sad. You are watching the evening news when the footage shows a cemetery; seeing this puts you in panic mode (or despair, or anger) because someone you knew well died suddenly and tragically before your eyes.

Hearing: Your next-door neighbor starts cutting the grass at 6:00 a.m. on Saturday when you are trying to sleep in, so you get irate. Your college roommate plays the same song over and over again, so you get frustrated and want to throw the speakers out the window. You heard a car's tailpipe backfire, so you are scared that someone is shooting a gun at you. Or, perhaps you might enjoy the relaxing sound of autonomous sensory meridian response (AMSR) soundtracks which may consist of very low-volume, feminine voices, or the crackling sound of a fireplace or a piece of paper being crumpled, or the sound of fingernails tapping on a table top. You can likely find free AMSR with a simple search on the Internet.

Smell: This sense is very strong, as you know when you smell certain foods which may bring you a sense of pleasant nostalgia or violent repulsion. Other examples could be, say, you pass by a group of people and you sense the smell of the same body lotion your ex-partner used, so you feel sadness because you miss them. Another is an example of when you smell cigarettes after recently quitting. The smell of cigarettes may trigger strong cravings to relapse (to go back to smoking).

Touch and taste: You get the point that experiencing certain things with your five senses can evoke memories, cravings, feelings, or emotions.

PLEASE START TO LEARN YOUR TRIGGERS NOW. In case you missed the above quote from Sun Tzu, please take the time to read it. Victory in your mental health battles!

4

# Using This Book

"If you change nothing, then nothing will change." -Unknown

How do you support someone who is struggling with mental health issues to find help for themselves? There is no certain answer here. Everyone is on a very personal journey towards management and treatment for their mental health issues. You can have empathy and be supportive during their journey to recovery with information from this book. The book offers insights into how individuals can find treatment options for their own mental health needs. It is a resource for anyone looking to address mental health challenges within their family or for themselves.

It is up to you how you use this book. For example, you could keep the book to help yourself. You could read the book first to provide support to the person you have in mind now. Alternatively, you may plan to present this book as a gift to that special someone while doing your frequent check-ins and offering your support. Perhaps you will be working with a group of people in a classroom, in a house of worship, at a mutual self-help group, or using it with your family at your home.

Whoever it is that you are helping or wherever you find yourself doing this, please remember that everyone is unique. One person may thrive by practicing breathing techniques while another person prefers to write a journal. It is essential to *invite* your person to participate because without their buy-in and consent, they might not want to be told what to do. Some will be resistant to trying new things in general, so use the rapport you have already built and perhaps demonstrate an activity before inviting them to participate with you. Some people may participate with you right away, but they may be just playing along to please you. At the very least, ask for honest feedback and be authentic as well. It may take time and extra effort doing the same activity to reach some relief.

I believe that RECOVERY is possible. Recovery is a *process* and it can take time. Just remember, *time takes time*. Once again. *Time takes time.* This is because of the time it takes for each individual to process things at their own speed. Likewise with every activity that you try in this book, it may not work the very first time because it is new and you're getting used to new things. For example when I was in graduate school, the professors would often start a class with a mindfulness exercise. Mindfulness takes practice and patience. Giving it my best, sincere efforts enabled that part of me to open up and grow. I was able to develop my self-awareness and my ability to stay grounded, or anchored, in the present moment. An ability to stay in the *Here and Now* can be an important step towards achieving a state of stability in your everyday life. When you can put everything else aside in order to accomplish your Here and Now thought process, then your tasks and your personal interactions with others can enjoy a richer life experience and you will enjoy life more knowing that you're fully engaged with yourself and with others. The ability to stay in the Here and Now may help you think more clearly, accomplish your tasks such as school work or running your business, and this could help with your ability to connect with people in your life to communicate more clearly to be understood and to be able to listen thoughtfully and empathize for a deeper understanding. One of the most important things one can do to maximize one's Mental Health is to be able to be vulnerable, truthful, and introspective about one's own needs, preferences, and goals. Start with your Here and Now.

One brief definition of recovery is "working on your healing and feeling better so that your functioning improves in your social, occupational, and educational aspects of life." Your therapeutic alliance with a mental health professional is an opportunity to set you up for success. Your professional helper can assess your mental health needs. Together, you can discuss your mental health goals, collaborate and establish your personal plan for you to work on your goals, to try to solve your problems, and to identify the barriers you are facing. It is essential that YOU set goals for YOUR recovery; your helping professional will guide you through the process.

It is important to communicate honestly with yourself. Please take the time to look below at the core feelings. Honestly, are you feeling one or more of these more or less often than you would like? Some of them are comfortable and pleasant for you while others are uncomfortable and unpleasant for you. Remember that you are human and these are normal feelings that live within us for life. We can try to push away or push down our feelings, but they are still with us. Eventually, they will rise again. So, practice sitting with your feelings without trying to "throw them" away, or trying to "throw them" at other people. Feelings and emotions are neither good nor bad; it's what you do with them that matters. Sitting with your anger might mean walking away from the situation that triggered your anger, and then going somewhere safe to breathe, grounding yourself, and letting the anger run its course. It is not fair to take out your feelings on someone else. It is not correct to blame others for your feelings because your feelings belong to you, not to them. Be compassionate with yourself and with others. So, you will be working on knowing yourself and keeping yourself grounded. There will be more on grounding later as you practice the exercises and activities in another chapter.

Anger

Fear

Happiness

Surprise

Sadness

Disgust

Some other well-known feelings.

Contentment

Resentment

Anticipation

Rage

Shame

Regret

Loneliness

Guilt

The hope is that you will consider taking these feelings that you find un-comfortable and unpleasant with you to your scheduled appointments with a helping professional. The work you do there is worth it because *you are worth it.*

# 5

# Overcoming Barriers

O vercoming barriers to mental health treatment can be challenging but is essential for well-being. One way is to seek support from your trusted friends or family who can help you find a therapist or counselor. Additionally, when you learn about mental health and treatment options, this can empower you to make informed decisions. It's important to reach out to healthcare professionals, clinics, or community organizations that offer affordable or sliding-scale services if cost is a barrier. Overcoming stigma and shame by talking openly about mental health can also make it easier to seek help. Remember, reaching out is a sign of strength, and there are resources available to support your journey towards better mental health. *You're worth it!*

Some people have said, "How can you help me if you haven't been in a situation like mine?" That is one of the major barriers for seeking help. My response to that is, "Doctors who haven't had cancer are treating cancer successfully. If you had cancer (or another illness), would you only want to be treated by a doctor who has also suffered and recovered from it?" I hope your answer is no, because people should get medical treatment when they are sick. Mental health treatment should be treated with the same seriousness as any other illness. Another key point is that people have empathy. They care about you. They want to help you take responsibility for your recovery. I urge you to have hope for your recovery journey.

There may be invisible barriers blocking your path to recovery such as social stigma, lack of financial means, and not knowing how or where to find professional help. You may be hesitant or embarrassed to seek professional help for your condition because of stigma. For some people, their culture and beliefs carry a sense of shame or people disapprove of seeking help from professional mental health providers. People living in such a culture fear social stigma if anyone were to learn about their problems and the fact that they are seeking help outside of their culturally approved ways of doing things, such as, "not talking about it," or "suck it up," or "it will go away if you (insert something here that is not professional mental health)." Rest assured, licensed professional helpers in the United States of America must abide by a code of ethics. The helper is obligated to maintain confidentiality to protect an adult's personal health information. Exceptions for disclosure might be, for example, parents need to know in order to care for their children. Disclosure may be mandatory, by ethics and/or by law, when a person provides specific information about plans and intentions to harm oneself (such as a suicide plan) or to harm others (such as homicide plan). Also, it is usually mandatory to report suspected abuse or neglect of children or elders.

Do you have barriers in finding helping professionals? Look for appropriate professional helpers in your local area such as licensed professional counselors, licensed clinical social workers, licensed psychologists, or a psychiatrist. A psychiatrist is a medical doctor

(M.D.) or a doctor of osteopathic medicine (D.O.) who specializes in the treatment of mental health conditions. A psychiatrist can prescribe medications indicated for a specific condition, such as depression or schizophrenia. A licensed nurse practitioner (N.P.) or physician's assistant (P.A) can also prescribe medications, depending on their scope of practice. There are also peer support specialists (PSS) who have lived-experience with their own mental health recovery; the PSS is an excellent resource in terms of providing a living example of successful recovery.. An example of scope of practice is that you should not go to a dermatologist (medical specialist who treats the skin) to seek a mental health medication. In many cases, you may visit your medication prescriber only for checkups for refills, while you will likely visit your psychologist, counselor, or clinical social worker more frequently for sessions that focus on the work you are doing for your recovery.

I strongly encourage you to make a plan to get professional help as soon as possible. Make that connection by seeking helping professionals in your area. If you have to take off work to attend a mental health appointment, keep your communications simple; you can simply tell your supervisor that you have a medical appointment, and leave out the details. Usually, you are not obligated to disclose the specifics of your medical appointments with your employer; check with your human resources department on what information your employer is allowed to ask you about your personal and medical situation.

As for what you tell other people in your life about your appointments, you can keep that private. Here is a way of setting a boundary without having to explain yourself. When someone (probably not your partner, though) gets nosey, rememberI the "rule of three." Simply answer their nosey question with broad-brush, factual information three times, for example, a co-worker asks, "Why did you take off work this morning?"

An example response could be, "I had a medical appointment." Then you stop talking. You could change the subject back to work related matters.

But then your co-worker asks a second time, "Why weren't you at work this morning?" Again, you answer, "I had a medical appointment."

Then, your co-worker asks a third time, "What's wrong with you that you had to miss work?" You answer, "I had a medical appointment."

This is usually when the nosey co-worker gives up and changes the subject. The point here is that you have the right to privacy and to keep your work life separate from your private life.

However, when you are talking with your helping professional, you can start to lower your boundaries. Once you are in the session with your helper, the hope is that you have been able to overcome most of your barriers to treatment. That helping person may ask you some questions you would never tell anyone. You may feel offended, but these questions are asked to help you figure out what might be a barrier to your recovery so that you can gain insights and work on solutions that work for your unique situation.

# 6

# Finding Your Helping Professional

There are different ways to find these mental health profession-als. For those who have health insurance, call your insurance company for details. Usually you can find their phone number on the back side of your insurance card, or you can find in-network and out-of-network providers on the insurance website or smart phone app. If you have Medicaid or Medicare, you can find more information from them by contacting them directly.

For those without insurance coverage, there are typically community mental health resources available in your local area. The cost to you may be at a sliding scale rate (lower cost depending on your income situation), and occasionally at no cost. Call them to find out if a case manager is available to assist you with your specific situation. This is the website for Mental Health America where you can find additional information: https://mhanational.org/bipoc-mental-health/community-care

Self-pay is an option to pay completely out of your own money for services. That means you would be hiring the helping professional at whichever rate you can negotiate and then you could pay with cash, credit card, or another financial service to transfer the money.

Veterans of the US armed forces may have several different options for finding helping professionals. Primarily, the Department of Veterans Affairs has its hospitals, outpatient clinics, and Vet Centers. Follow this link for more information: https://www.va.gov/find-locations/ . Select "VA Health" and then, "service type" and then select "mental health care."

There are many Veterans Services Organizations (VSO) that are non-profit organizations that advocate and serve Veterans in the community. The VSO is not going to have helping professionals on staff, but they may be able to direct you to resources in your area. The Department of Veterans Affairs has a list of recognized VSOs on their website: https://www.va.gov/ogc/recognizedvsos.asp

Each US state or territory will usually have its own office, agency, department, foundation, advocate, or commission of Veterans affairs. Search for accredited VSOs by state or territory here: https://www.va. gov/ogc/apps/accreditation/index.asp?

This is not an exhaustive list, but you may have learned about some of these VSOs in the news, television commercials, or billboard signs: The Wounded Warrior Project, AMVETS, Veterans of Foreign Wars, American Legion, Jewish War Veterans of the USA, Paralyzed Veterans of America, and Vietnam Veterans of America.

Students enrolled at a community college or at a university may have access to an on-campus counseling center. These counseling centers might not charge fees for services; please check with your counseling center to find out more.

Your workplace may have an Employee Assistance Program (EAP). Your job may have a website that provides a phone number to call for this service. In a larger company, the human resources office may have information if your employer has an EAP.

While you are seeking a professional helper, be discreet in asking in your social circles or with colleagues at work. Word of mouth is an excellent way of finding referrals, however, take caution in taking casual referrals to maintain your confidentiality. While it is important to break down the stigma of mental illness and treatment for it, please be mindful of your right to privacy.

In summary, your health is important. You have the right to seek treatment for both physical and mental health concerns. Take care of yourself and make contact with a professional mental health helper. *You're worth it!*

7

# Start with Self-Care, the Core

"Decide what kind of life you really want, and then say no to everything that isn't that." -Unknown

Self-care means taking time to do things that make you feel good, both physically and emotionally. It's like filling up your "gas tank," so you can get back on the road to wellness to be your best self. Self-care can include simple things like getting enough sleep, eating nutritious food, and staying active. It's also about taking breaks when you need them and finding ways to relax, like reading a book or talking to a friend. Self-care is important because it helps you stay healthy, happy, and better able to handle life's challenges. It's like taking care of a precious plant – when you nurture yourself, you can bloom and grow into your full potential.

One step at a time. Let's look at basic needs and motivation. In the 1940s, American psychologist Abraham Maslow taught us his way of thinking about how human beings are motivated. He created a pyramid to demonstrate that the base of the pyramid must be achieved before a person can work towards adding higher levels to the pyramid. At the base of the pyramid are your must-have basic needs.

Be sure your basic needs are being met so you can optimize your mental health self-management. The things your body must have first are food, water, rest, and staying warm. After those needs are met come physical protection and security. After that, we need to feel a sense of belonging and love. After that, we need esteem and respect. Last, we will eventually yearn for self-actualization, or reaching your full potential as a human being. My hope now is that you are making yourself physically comfortable, that you are in a safe environment, and that you look at yourself with kindness and compassion as you move forward. Remember, you are a unique individual, thus it might be wise to limit your comparison to others as they might not be in the same situation as you are.

Self-care is all about taking care of yourself physically and emotionally. One way to practice self-care is by setting aside some quiet time each day to relax and clear your mind. You can do this by meditating, deep breathing, or simply sitting in a peaceful place. This helps reduce stress and improve your mental well-being. Another idea is to get moving! Exercise is a great way to take care of your body. Whether it's going for a walk, dancing to your favorite music, or playing a sport you love, being active can boost your mood and energy levels.

Eating well is another important part of self-care. Make sure to nourish your body with nutritious foods that give you energy and help you feel your best. Staying hydrated by drinking plenty of water is also essential. Don't forget to get enough sleep. A good night's rest is like a reset button for your body and mind. Finally, reach out to friends and family for support when you're feeling down. Talking to someone you trust can be a great way to relieve stress and share your feelings. Remember, taking care of yourself is important, and it's okay to prioritize your well-being.

In the introduction, I discussed the importance of personal hygiene, nutrition, and safety, as well. I would like to emphasize those aspects of overall self-management, not only for mental health self-management. Each time you complete any aspect of your self-care, whether it is just getting out of bed or going for a 30-minute walk, please celebrate your success with a silent, "good job!" *You are worth it.*

8

# Individual Self-Management Skills

These are readings, recommendations of activities, and healthy coping skills that you can practice to start your journey towards mental health self-management.

## ASK FOR HELP

You might think you are a burden to others. You may think it is too late, but it's not! Isolating yourself is not a solution, so reach out to others for socialization. See the resources section for more.

## SELF-SOOTHING

The goal here is to start learning skills to feel a little better, self-soothing, before you make it into the professional helper's session. You can keep these healthy skills in your "tool bag" to use forever. You can even offer some of these to others who are open to trying them. That said, triggers can be complex, so you will need to identify your triggers while working on healthy skills to self-soothe (eventually using these skills without help from anybody else). I recommend working with a helping professional as soon as you can to address trigger issues with appropriate interventions. You will find various activities below that may help with your triggers. It can help to remove yourself from triggers, such as walking away from arguing or unpleasant strangers, stepping away from drama in your personal life, doing breathing exercises, doing stress-relief activities, etc.

IMPORTANT: People cutting their skin with razors or other sharp objects for "relief" will likely need immediate medical attention. Self-harm is NOT self-soothing behavior.

SLEEP (for mood and daily functioning)

Sleep is essential.  If you are not sleeping enough, this will affect your health, your mood, and your behavior. It is a skill to maintain a consistent time (at night) to go to sleep and a consistent time to wake up (in the morning).  Keeping it consistent can help to stabilize your mood. Have you noticed how young children behave when they are well-rested? If you are the kind of person without a bedtime, I recommend you work on this skill. When a person is having trouble sleeping, the recommendation here is to learn and practice "sleep hygiene." This is a routine to get you ready to sleep and to create a healthier sleep environment. An example of someone's sleep hygiene routine might be to drink only 16 ounces of coffee in the morning and then stop drinking or eating anything with caffeine in it for the rest of the day. They make their bedroom cool and dark during sleeptime. They remove the television from their bedroom.  They only read books in a chair that is separated from the bed/bedroom, never reading in bed.  An hour before they get into bed, they stop using all electronic devices with screens.  They take a bath or shower.  Then, every night at the same exact time, they get into bed, turn out the lights, put their head on the pillow, and breathe deeply until falling asleep. Of course there are different ways to make your routine. You will find yours. If your routine does not work after two weeks, ask your helping professionals for assistance.

THE GRATITUDE JAR (for depression, anxiety, grieving, obsessive-compulsive behaviors, anger, racing thoughts, or most anything)

Use a clean jar or bowl as a container. Write one statement of gratitude every morning on a small slip or piece of paper. For example, "I am grateful to have running water." or "I am grateful that my neighbor lent me a cup of sugar yesterday." Write it. Fold the paper. Place it into your jar. Your statements can be anything of value to you. At the end of the day, read your statement aloud to yourself. Contemplate gratitude for two minutes. Collect your statements for a week and read them all on the seventh day. You may even keep collecting for a month.

THINKING DIFFERENTLY (for almost all issues)

-Learn to change from one season to the next. Just as we have the four seasons, Spring, Summer, Autumn, and Winter, your life will have its "seasonal changes.". Some changes may seem small to you, but large to someone else. For example, development from childhood to adulthood, or graduation from a school to finding your first job, or raising children to becoming an empty-nester, or the loss of a loved one. You will have lived the experiences of your own unique changes and perhaps something is coming to mind right now.

-Acceptance of the closing of a season can be a difficult process as another season begins. Acceptance of the change is a step forward. Commit to a healthy attitude, to making plans for your best life, and live your life with positive intention in the new season. Be patient. Patience may be easier said than done. Think about it like this: the best way to forget is to remember. So that you can draw lessons from the past, it is important to accept it. If you are intent on wanting to forget what has happened as soon as possible, you will likely end up filled with feelings of anxiety. Give yourself time.

-Forgive yourself and forgive others. We regret the many mistakes we have made and we would like to turn back the clock, but time travel to the past is not possible. Instead of punishing yourself for how things have happened, instead try to forgive yourself and to learn lessons from it. Likewise, you must free yourself from bitter feelings towards those who have done you harm so that you can move on to better things in life. Use positive words and thoughts for yourself and others. Supposedly the ancient sage, Buddha said, "What you think, you become. What you feel, you attract. What you imagine, you create." For example, instead of saying "I can't..." use "I prefer..." etc. How could you reframe your language to say what you mean in a neutral or positive way, especially when talking about yourself?

-Let go. It is not always possible to understand everything that has happened to us. There will be unanswered questions. Let go of everything that is not under your control.

-Saying "goodbye." Have you had a chance to grieve over the relationship that ended, or that person who departed this world, or that job you don't have anymore? You *do have* the right to feel anger, sadness, or despair for a certain time. Sit with your feelings for a little while and then *talk* about them instead of suppressing your pain. You are feeling what other humans are capable of feeling, so trust that others can relate and can empathize and can connect with you, such as family, friends, and helping professionals. Next, accept your change of season. It is time to say goodbye to what you have lost. Then you can start to welcome this new season in your life.

BREATHING EXERCISES (stress, anxiety, depression, fear, anger, disgust, surprise, guilt, shame, etc.)

-4X4 (four-by-four) Breathing. Sit down in a comfortable chair or lie down on your bed if you think you might fall asleep. We are simply counting to four as we breathe in, hold, and exhale. Thereby, breathe into your nostrils for four seconds. Hold for four seconds. Exhale for four seconds. Pause breathing for four no more than seconds. Continue for no more than two minutes at a time before taking a break.

-Diaphragmatic breathing. Stand (or sit upright) with your back against the wall, clasp your hands together, and stretch upwards, while breathing in and out slowly and deeply for one or two minutes. This helps many people to calm down, focus, and relax enough to get ready for sleep.

-The Expanding Balloon. Sit comfortably in a safe location. Look around at the space surrounding your body. Also look around at the space in the room or at the location where you are now. You could possibly be outside. Inhale, breathing air into your lungs so that your belly rises a bit. Now, as you exhale, imagine you have a balloon expanding from your body. Continue to inhale normally, and then your outward breaths inflate the imaginary balloon, little by little, until it fills the room (or the imaginary balloon reaches a boundary you have selected if you are outside). Feel free to deflate the imaginary balloon slowly with your breaths as well.

-Breathe above the storm. Sit or lie down in a safe, comfortable place. If you are able to close your eyes, this may be helpful because this activity is using your calm breathing while using your imagination. You are going to practice being calm, composed, and steady. First, you will breathe, inhaling and exhaling in this calm, safe place. Know that you are safe here in this place and that you can return to this place wherever you want. Next, in your imagination, picture a storm. Maintain your smooth, steady breaths while you imagine yourself rising above the storm, watching the storm as you continue distancing yourself from the high winds, lightning, and chaos. As you look upon the storm below, you are safe, steady, and able to observe it without being affected by it. You control your breathing. You can watch the storm from a distance while keeping an awareness of the actual present moment. Practice this exercise often. Practice in your imagination may serve you well in remaining calmer and steadier when the real world seems to become difficult, confusing, or hectic.

## ENERGIZE YOURSELF

-Blast Off! Do you have trouble getting out of bed due to depression? How about when you're sitting in a chair, but you're just "not feeling it," so you blow off household chores or even a gathering of friends? With this exercise, imagine you are a rocket on the launchpad to fly into outer space. If that rocketship doesn't work for you, perhaps you're an airplane taking off for a vacation. Perhaps you can imagine yourself as an arrow being pulled into the bow to be launched at a bullseye. Think of something that works for you, but also picture where you will be going in the real world once you've launched out of your bed/chair. Could it be you are launching to go into the bathroom to brush your teeth? Could it be you are launching to go to work? Could it be you are launching to get something to eat or drink? With the images in mind of what you will be doing, countdown 10-9-8-7-6-5-4-3-2-1-ZERO! Move your body to the best of your ability. Blast off!

-Clap! Clap! Clap! Feeling down? Bored? No motivation? If you are in a place with the freedom to move, make some noise, and even sing, you can clap your hands-create energy for feeling more upbeat or motivated to do what you want to do! What song do you know with a good beat? Imagine hearing the drums, the bass, the rhythm, and the song's energy flowing through you. Now can you clap your hands to that beat? If you have the ability you could turn on some music on your smartphone or radio.

-Laughter yoga. Laughter Yoga was created by an Indian physician named Dr. Madan Kataria. Several years ago, I had the pleasure of meeting Slash Coleman, a US Laughter Ambassador who had studied with Dr. Kataria in India. As luck would have it, Slash came to facilitate Laughter Yoga groups where I was working at the time. He taught us about the benefits of laughter, whether it's forced, fake, or real. Laughter for several minutes at a time can help lift our moods, as well as increase our lung capacity over time. I encourage you to laugh, perhaps practice your fake laughing at home, and then attend a Laughter Yoga event near you. The activities are fun, silly, creative, imaginative, and spirit-lifting! You can find Slash Coleman on LinkedIn, Instagram, and Wikipedia! I encourage you to browse the web page for Laughter Yoga International to find an event near you. Links will be in the resources section of the book.

GROUNDING AND RELIEF

-Use a calendar to plan and track activities. Perhaps this can help you feel more in control of your plans and to see some of your accomplishments written down to review.

-Five things. This is an exercise to practice when you are feeling neutral. You can use this exercise when you are starting to become irritated, have racing thoughts, or are unable to focus. It may also work to ground you when you feel overwhelmed. Practicing Five Things can help you remember to use it when you need it. First, stop at a safe place to focus on what you are doing. Breathe with intention. First, say aloud five things you can SEE with your eyes as you look around your environment. Keep breathing. Next, say aloud five things you can hear in your environment. Keep breathing. Next, say five things aloud that you can feel with your sense of touch. You may wiggle your toes or reach out with your hands to touch some things that are safe and appropriate to touch in your environment, such as your clothing, your hair, the seat of your chair, or something in your purse or pocket. Keep breathing. Continue with four things you can see, four things you can hear, and four things you can feel. The four things can be from the group of the five things you just mentioned. Keep breathing. Continue similarly with three things. Keep breathing. Two things. Keep breathing. Finally, name one thing. You are done with the exercise. Notice

-Nature walk. Hopefully you have some green spaces or nature near you to visit. This is a time to turn off your electronic devices for a few minutes so you can connect to the natural world. As you are walking use your five senses. Look closely at the plants, rocks, and skies. Listen closely to the birds, the breeze, and any other sounds. Breathe and notice any scents. If you know it's safe (and legal), touch a tree, a rock, or some grass. Even five minutes outdoors with this mindset can be helpful in staying in the present moment to clear away stressful thoughts or clear the mental cobwebs that block your productivity. (This can also be done with another person or a dog.)

-The Orange. This may be a seasonal activity due to the availability of oranges in your area. However, this can be done with your imagination or you may be able to find a suitable replacement food that meets your dietary needs and the purpose of this activity. With an unpeeled orange, (perhaps a plate, napkins, and water to clean your hands) have a seat in a safe, comfortable place. Perhaps place a yoga mat, towel, or quilt on the ground at a quiet park or under a tree. You are going to slow down your activity considerably to stay in the moment. First, simply hold the unpeeled orange to feel its temperature, texture, and weight. Consider the growth process for an orange from blossom to this citrus delight. Next, look at its colors, textures, and perfection or imperfections. Does the peel shine in the light or is it dull? How does the color of the orange contrast with the environment? Next, hold the unpeeled orange to your nose and try to smell it. What do you notice now? Are there other smells in your environment as well? Next, place the unpeeled orange on the mat or towel in front of you. Consider the possible place of origin of this orange. Wonder with curiosity about the hands that may have picked it. Consider the voyage this orange took to arrive where you are now. Next, take the orange in your hands again. Do this next step slowly. Are you able to tear open the peel just a tiny bit so that you can smell its inner fragrance? What are you noticing as you see the small bit of peel removed and its inner fragrance revealed? How does the fragrance of this orange compare to other fragrances and odors you know? Now, slowly, and carefully peel the rest of the orange without eating it. Continue to use your senses as you did earlier when the orange was not yet peeled. Now, take your first, small bite. Slowly chew and taste it. Enjoy the rest of the fruit as you wish. Just remember to clean up the mess. Enjoy. (This activity can also be done with another person.)

-Progressive Muscle Relaxation (PMR). To practice, sit or lie down in a safe, comfortable place. Breathe as smoothly and steadily as you can. Close your eyes if you are able. You will be slowly and consciously making a small muscle or group of muscles in your body tight for just an instant, and then releasing the muscles before moving on to the next muscles. Skip any areas of the body that are injured or too painful to make tense. Just notice those areas and move on to the next muscle areas. Start with tightening or clenching your toes for three seconds and then releasing the tension. Notice the feeling of the relaxation in that area. Next, tighten muscles in your feet for three seconds and then release the tension. Notice how you feel. Continue to do this through your ankles, calves, knees, thighs, pelvic floor,buttocks, abdomen, chest, shoulders, biceps, forearms, hands, neck, smiling muscles, eye muscles, and forehead. Once you have completed this circuit of muscles, continue breathing smoothly while you notice your entire body. What are you noticing? Feel free to reverse the circuit. PMR can help with grounding you as well as preparing you for sleep.

-The Waves. Practice by lying down in a safe, comfortable place. If you can close your eyes, you will be imagining gentle ocean waves as you imagine yourself observing the water from the beach. As you inhale slowly, see the waters rising to a crest as they approach the shore. As you release your breath to exhale slowly, your imaginary waves break and the foamy waters flow onto the beach and then they recede back into the ocean. Continue breathing and making waves for two minutes at a time.

-Go Limp. The goal here is to de-stress your entire body. Practice by lying down or sitting in a safe, comfortable place. Let all of your muscles go limp, like spaghetti. Breathe and imagine hard, dry pasta noodles, sinking into a pot of water and going soft and supple. Practice can help you learn to notice when your body is becoming tense. Then perhaps you can learn to de-stress those specific muscles with just a thought and breathing.

-Anti-kegels. The goal here is to de-stress your entire body. After some practice, this may come in handy while you are trying to focus and stay in the moment. For example, when you are seated in a learning or business setting, this may help with focus, attention, and may increase learning capacity. It may even improve a student's test performance if used in the classroom, while studying, and during the exam. (It worked for me.) With your thoughts, can you squint your eyes and then release those muscles? With this exercise, you will practice using the power of your thoughts to release the tension in a certain group of muscles to start a chain reaction of relaxation. Kegels are contractions and release of your pelvic floor muscles. To find your pelvic floor muscles, stop the flow of your urine for just a second when you next go to the bathroom. Now that you know your pelvic floor, practice by lying down or sitting in a safe, comfortable place. Breathe normally and use the power of your mind to locate and release those pelvic floor muscles. Continue to breathe and imagine those muscles softening. The rest of your body should follow suit with a wave of released tension.

-Field of View Expansion. The goal here is to de-stress your entire body. After some practice, this may come in handy while you are trying to focus and stay in the moment. For example, when you are seated in a learning or business setting, using this may help with focus, attention, and may increase learning capacity. It may even improve a student's test performance if used in the classroom, while studying, and during the exam. (It worked for me.) Practice by standing or sitting in a safe, comfortable place. Look softly at a specific spot on the wall ahead of you. Now, breathe steadily as you are looking at that spot, and then open your field of view to include your peripheral vision, meaning you should be able to see everything ahead of you and be able to perceive out to approximately 170 degrees to the sides. If this helps, imagine you are standing in front of the goal at a football/soccer field, looking across the field at the other goal. As you look at the center of the goal, without turning your head, open your vision so that you can see the fans in the stands on either side of the goal ahead of you.

## ADDICTION

Self-management for addictions is all about learning to take control of your actions and make healthier choices. When someone struggles with addiction, like to drugs, alcohol, or even things like video games, it can be really tough to break free. But self-management means setting goals for yourself, like cutting back on the addictive behavior or even quitting altogether, and then finding ways to stick to those goals. It's important to identify triggers that make you want to engage in the addictive behavior and figure out ways to avoid or cope with those triggers. Surrounding yourself with supportive friends and seeking help from professionals can also be part of self-management. Remember, it's a journey, and it may not be easy, but with determination and support, you can make positive changes in your life and overcome addiction.

There are people who want to help you in this battle. Please refer to the resources for SAMHSA, NAMI, and ABAM. Also look for mutual self-help groups. Call and/or use your computer or phone to reach out to them now to connect with people who can teach you how to fight this battle against addiction. You will likely find people living in recovery who can show you that you can do it, too. Still, consider using the skills listed in this book. *You are worth it.*

9

# Other Skills, Activities, Suggestions

The list below is for your consideration to include into your self-care repertoire. Some can be individual and others could be done in a group.

-Music. Listen to your tunes! Learn an instrument if you don't already play one. Sing by yourself (in the car or in the shower) or join a singing group or a choir.

-Art. Visit a museum. Learn to paint, draw, sculpt clay, or create your own art. Visit one of the many hobby and arts and crafts stores in your area.

-Read more. Find your favorite genre, such as fiction, biographies, non-fiction, etc. Join a book club to meet people who are sharing your reading experiences. Living vicariously through written stories may be helpful for changing your thinking for a while.

-Mandala coloring book and colored pencils or pens. These are excellent for adults and children. Many stores sell these at various prices.

I recommend coloring for grounding or relieving anxiety. Coloring is great almost anytime you are looking for something to do.

-Write a journal of your activities and reflections. I recommend this for almost anyone to process your life and to get to know yourself better. You may want to show parts of this to your mental health provider when you are ready.

-Declutter your home, work spaces, and yard. A sense of a healthier and more organized environment can improve your frame of mind.

-Schedule your time and make a routine for every day. It is okay to make time for yourself to be alone to work on personal projects for some time, but start using a calendar. The calendar is a tool that many people are not using to its full capacity. Using a calendar may provide you a sense of peace and stability up to a certain point. It can help you to schedule self-care events, to schedule socialization events, to remember medical appointments, and to track your everyday successes.

-Volunteer your time. Once you have established stability in your overall well-being, helping others (including animals and plants) can increase your mental health and self-management when you do this regularly. This is because most volunteering involves a connection to others. That feeling you get is real. For example, spending time at a retirement home with people who need more social interaction or participating in a neighborhood farming project.

-Surround yourself with people who promote positivity, success, and safety. Where might you find such people? Some examples are:

-Exercise at the Gym or at a fitness club

-Outdoor activities, gardening, walking, hiking, biking
-Yoga
-Laughter Yoga
-Tai Chi
-Going to peaceful religious services
-Cooking/baking classes
-Foreign language classes
-Your favorite hobbies that you may have forgotten!

Investing in your mental health and overall wellness is a worthwhile journey that can result in a happier, more balanced life. By learning coping skills and engaging in healthy activities, you will be more prepared to tackle life's challenges with resilience and grace. The tools that you choose to pick up and use can help you work your life with an improved capacity to manage stress, anxiety, and emotional upset more confidently and effectively. Whether it's a mindful exercise, regular exercise, or seeking professional help, when you take steps towards mental health self-management can unlock a world of positive outcomes, emotional stability, improved relationships, and a greater sense of life satisfaction. Walk down the path to mental health and wellness, as it is a more pleasant journey towards your own happiness and well-being. *You're worth it!*

# 10

# Conclusion

That person who put this book into your hands cares about you! Your mental health self-management is a journey that both the person who bought this book and the person struggling with their mental health can embark upon together. Life has its challenges, but together you can work on tackling them. Whether you are a friend, family member, or mental health professional, you play an important role in offering support, understanding, and encouragement. Lend your listening ear, create a safe space for open communication, and point your person in the right direction to find helpful resources.

For the person facing mental health challenges, self-management is about learning to recognize your emotions, thoughts, and triggers. It involves seeking help when you need it, practicing self-care, and developing coping strategies. You're allowed to ask for help; it's a sign of strength, not weakness.

There is a hope here that your new insights from this book can break down the barriers that you perceive that mental health issues may present. I hope you will take good care of yourself now because YOU

ARE WORTH IT! I hope that you will start feeling better, become motivated to get treatment, and to enter into recovery. I want you to live your best life, hoping that some of this book's basic information and skills for mental health self-management have given you some inspiration. Even if you skipped chapters, some of the information and skills presented may have helped you to self-soothe or get out of a funk. By now, another hope is that you have already reached out to schedule an appointment with a professional helper. Recovery is possible.

Wishing you wellness!

# 11

# Resources

988 Suicide & Crisis Lifeline. (n.d.). *988 Suicide & Crisis Lifeline.* 988 Suicide & Crisis Lifeline. https://988lifeline.org/

*Addiction isn't a weakness, but recovery takes strength | NAMI: National Alliance on Mental Illness.* (n.d.). https://www.nami.org/Press-Media/In-The-News/2021/Addiction-Isn-t-a-Weakness-but-Recovery-Takes-Strength

AirlineCareer.com. (2017, December 12). *PA announcements study Guide - AirlineCareer.com.* https://airlinecareer.com/tests/pa-announcements-study-guide/

Bennadi, D. (2014). Self-medication: A current challenge. *Journal of Basic and Clinical Pharmacy, 5*(1), 19. https://doi.org/10.4103/0976-0105.128253

*Child protective Services | childcare.gov.* (n.d.). https://childcare.gov/consumer-education/child-protective-services#:~:text=If%20you%20suspect%20that%20a,800%2D422%2D4453%20immediately

*Community care.* (n.d.). Mental Health America. https://mhanational.org/bipoc-mental-health/community-care

Counsel, O. O. G. (n.d.). *VA.gov | Veterans Affairs.* https://www.va.gov/ogc/recognizedvsos.asp

Davis, J. L. (2004, March 23). *How to find a therapist*. WebMD. https://www.webmd.com/mental-health/features/how-to-find-thera pist

*Domestic Violence Support | National Domestic Violence Hotline*. (2023, April 27). The Hotline. https://www.thehotline.org/

*Find help*. (n.d.). https://www.samhsa.gov/find-help

*Find VA locations | Veterans Affairs*. (n.d.). Veterans Affairs. https://w ww.va.gov/find-locations/

Gunnell, D., Appleby, L., Arensman, E., Hawton, K., John, A., Kapur, N., Khan, M. M., O'Connor, R. C., Pirkis, J., Caine, E. D., Chan, L. F., Chang, S., Chen, Y., Christensen, H., Dandona, R., Eddleston, M., Erlangsen, A., Harkavy–Friedman, J., Kirtley, O. J., . . . Yip, P. (2020). Suicide risk and prevention during the COVID-19 pandemic. *The Lancet Psychiatry, 7*(6), 468–471. https://doi.org/10.1016/s2215-0366(20)301 71-1

*How to ask for help in your recovery when everyone's struggling | NAMI: National Alliance on Mental Illness*. (n.d.). https://www.nami.org/Press-Media/In-The-News/2021/How-to-Ask-for-Help-in-Your-Recovery-When-Everyone-s-Struggling

International Association for Suicide Prevention. (2023, August 18). *Suicidal Crisis Support - IASP*. IASP. https://www.iasp.info/suicidalthou ghts/

Kataria, M. (n.d.). *Laughter Yoga International - Health, happiness and world Peace*. Laughter Yoga International. https://www.laughteryoga.o rg/

Levreau, D. (n.d.). *Find a physician*. https://www.abam.net/find-a-ph ysician

Mcleod, S., PhD. (2023a). Maslow's hierarchy of needs. *Simply Psychology*. https://www.simplypsychology.org/maslow.html

Mcleod, S., PhD. (2023b). Maslow's hierarchy of needs. *Simply Psychology*. https://www.simplypsychology.org/maslow.html

*NAPSA – National Adult Protective Services Association.* (n.d.). https://www.napsa-now.org/

*SAMHSA's national helpline.* (n.d.). SAMHSA. https://www.samhsa.gov/find-help/national-helpline

Suni, E., & Suni, E. (2023). Mastering Sleep Hygiene: Your path to quality sleep. *Sleep Foundation.* https://www.sleepfoundation.org/sleep-hygiene

Wallacker, B. E., & Griffith, S. B. (2008). *Sun Tzu: The Art of War.* https://catalog.umj.ac.id/index.php?p=show_detail&id=62408

Website, N. (2023, March 23). *8 tips for healthy eating.* nhs.uk. https://www.nhs.uk/live-well/eat-well/how-to-eat-a-balanced-diet/eight-tips-for-healthy-eating/

Wikipedia contributors. (2022). Slash Coleman. *Wikipedia.* https://en.wikipedia.org/wiki/Slash_Coleman